21 DAYS
to a Spiritual Makeover

JOURNEY TO A CONSECRATED LIFE

SUGANTHI SAM

CONTENTS

Introduction

D id you know that it's God's desire for us to have a life filled with peace, joy, wholeness, and prosperity in every way? This is so true, in fact, that God has made this abundant life a reality through Jesus Christ, our Lord, who loves us and gave Himself for us. Hallelujah!

Many believers, however, walk in shame, guilt, and hopelessness, feeling defeated and worthless. It's true that we're in an unseen battle, but the unseen battle we're in is with a defeated enemy, so we need to arise to walk in what is rightfully ours!

This devotional will give you a fresh start to walking in abundant life by recommitting every part of your life to God. It can also be used as a step-by-step and day-by-day guide to go from glory to glory. As well, the confessions in each devotion will help you to decree the blessings and promises of God into your life.

The Name and the Blood of Jesus is more than enough and His Word is powerful to do what God is intended to do in our lives. To God be all the glory!

Yesterday is history; tomorrow is a mystery. Let's focus on today, which is right before us!

"And the Lord--who is the Spirit--makes us more and more likehimaswearechangedintohisgloriousimage." 2 Corinthians 3:18

Dedication

I dedicate this devotional to my loving Lord and Savior Jesus Christ, my beloved husband Sam Dewald, and my precious kids, Immanuel and Irene.

1
A Set-Apart Life

"Consecrate yourselves therefore, and be holy, for I am the Lord." Leviticus 20:7

"Sanctify yourselves, for tomorrow the Lord will do wonders among you." Joshua 3:5

To be consecrated simply means that you've set yourself apart from evil, have turned to God, and are prepared to be used by Him. When we receive Jesus as our Savior, we are cleansed and made holy. It also means that we have to decide, on a daily basis, to consecrate ourselves and walk away from evil and worldly desires.

Romans 12:1-2 says:

"I beseech you therefore, brethren, by the mercies of God, that you present your bodies a living sacrifice, holy, acceptable to God, which is your reasonable service. 2 And do not be conformed to this world, but be transformed by the renewing of your mind, that you may prove what is that good and acceptable and perfect will of God."

Likewise, 2 Corinthians 7:1 states that since we have His promises, we need to *"cleanse ourselves from all defilement of flesh and spirit, perfecting holiness in the fear of God."* If we want God to use us in these end times, it takes consecration and preparation, both inside and out!

Take a minute to think about the following question:

What is distracting me from following the Lord and living for Him wholeheartedly? Write it down. Ask the Lord to help you today!

Confession:

My body is a temple for the Holy Spirit, and I've been redeemed, cleansed, and sanctified by the blood of Jesus. I present my body as a living sacrifice, holy and acceptable to God. My body is for the Lord, and the Lord is for my body. The devil has no place in me, no power over me, and no unsettled claims against me. All has been settled by the blood of Jesus. I renew my mind by the Word of God and the truth sanctifies me. I yield my spirit to God and He sanctifies me by His Spirit. Now may the God of peace himself sanctify me completely, and my whole spirit and soul and body be kept blameless at the coming of our Lord Jesus Christ (1 Corinthians 6:19; Hebrews 10:10,13; Romans 12:1,2; Revelation 12:11; Romans 12:3; John 17:17, 1 Thessalonians 5:23).

Notes:

2
Watch Over Your Eye Gate

To live a consecrated (set apart) life is a decision that has to be made by every believer, every single day! God warns us to watch over the gates of our bodies. In today's devotion, we'll discuss what's often referred to as the *"eye gate."*

In Luke 11:34, Jesus teaches about the eye being the lamp of the body. He states that *"when your eyes are healthy, your whole body also is full of light. But when they are unhealthy, your body also is full of darkness."*

Take a moment and think what you're allowing your eyes to look at. Ask yourself the following questions:

- Are the things I'm letting in through my eyes glorifying God?
- Are they helping me to grow closer to Him, or are they stealing the purity of my thoughts and dragging me slowly into perverted, ungodly desires?
- Am I longing for God's presence or giving myself excuses to stay away from His holy presence?

Only you can answer these questions, and no one is responsible for the choices you make. If you are serious about getting closer to God and being filled with His presence continuously, then hear His gentle yet powerful nudging today. He is speaking to you, and He wants you to hear Him today!

Ask the Lord to help you the moment you are tempted to watch anything that isn't pure in His sight. Shut down your computer. Turn off your television. Turn your eyes away from billboards with perverted advertisements. Close any magazines filled with nudity and sex. These are all ways you can help watch over your eye gate.

May the Lord strengthen your spiritual eyes as you decide

to consecrate your physical eyes today! It's time to possess the promises of the Lord for your life. Don't trade your everlasting blessings and treasures for a moment of pleasure. It's not worth it!

> *"I have made a covenant with my eyes; How then could I gaze at a virgin?" Job 31:1*

> *"I will set no wicked thing before mine eyes: I hate the work of them that turn aside; it shall not cleave to me." Psalm 101:3*

> *"Wash and make yourselves clean. Take your evil deeds out of my sight; stop doing wrong" Isaiah 1:16*

Confession:

My hearing ear and the seeing eye, the Lord has made them both. My eye is the lamp of my body. My eyes are healthy, and so my whole body also is full of light. I will not set any wicked thing before my eyes: I hate the work of them that turn aside; it shall not cleave to me. I will allow the Word of God to wash me clean. I will take evil deeds out of my sight and will stop doing wrong. I will not have haughty eyes and a proud heart. I have made a covenant with my eyes; how then could I gaze at a virgin/young man? I lift up my eyes to the hills, from where does my help come? My help comes from the Lord, who made heaven and earth. Open my eyes, Lord, that I may behold wondrous things out of your law. Enlighten the eyes of my heart, that I may know what is the hope to which You have called me and the riches of Your glorious inheritance in the saints (Proverbs 20:12; Luke 11:34; Psalm 101:3; Isaiah 1:16; Proverbs 21:4; Job 31:1; Psalm 121:1; Psalm 119:18; Ephesians 1:18).

Notes:

3

Watch Over Your Ear Gate

"Whose report will you believe? I shall believe the report of the Lord..." This is the song ringing in my ears as I am writing today's devotion. In today's devo, we'll focus on the "ear gate."

Media is filled with negative news, and songs and programs filled with violence, uncertainty, terror, fear, obscene words, etc. are constantly filling our ears wherever we go. Although we cannot avoid being exposed to these things, since we live in this world, we need to remember that we're not of this world (John 17:14). It's important that we learn how to prepare ourselves to become victors and not victims. Yes, it's possible! Through Christ Jesus, all things are possible to us!

Romans 10:17 says that faith comes from hearing, and hearing through the word of God. Fear, the opposite of faith, comes by hearing the reports of the kingdom of darkness. For example, just hearing some advertisements promoting medications and their side effects can bring fear of sickness and death.

The best way to keep our hearts and minds protected from all fears and lies of the enemy is to tune our ears to hear God's voice and incline ourselves to His Word.

"Incline your ear, and come to me; hear, that your soul may live; and I will make with you an everlasting covenant, my steadfast, sure love..." Isaiah 55:3

Opening our ears to ungodly discussions and gossiping can also hinder our 'hearing' when God speaks. Today, decide to not allow your ears to become a dumpster open to negative trash. Instead, incline your ear to listen to His Word and to Him speaking to you.

Take a minute to think, repent, and ask Him to forgive and circumcise your ears. Consecrate your ears to the Lord so you can hear Him and live victoriously.

Confession:

I apply the blood of Jesus on the lobe of my ears. I have circumcised ears, and I will always yield to the Holy Spirit. My ears are opened. I will diligently listen to the voice of the Lord my God and do what is right in His eyes. I give ear to His commandments and keep all His statutes. I will hear what God the Lord will speak, for He will speak peace to me. I will diligently obey the voice of the Lord my God and I will be blessed according to His promises. I will be a doer of His word, and not a hearer only. I will hear a word behind me, saying, *"This is the way, walk in it"*, and I will and walk and be victorious (Leviticus 8:23; Acts 7:51; Psalm 40:6; Exodus 15:26; Psalm 58:8; Deuteronomy 28:1; James 1:22, Isaiah 30:21).

Notes:

4

The Most Important Tool of Your Body

Recently, a friend of mine said something hurtful about me. I was hurt so deeply and that it almost knocked me down. By God's grace, I was able to overcome, and I have the victory!

I'm sure you've had many similar bumps in your walk with the Lord. What I love about God is that He even heals us from wounds caused by other people's words. Today, we'll be talking about the most important tool of your body, which is your mouth. I certainly believe today's devotional will bless you as it did me!

Physical power enters our body through our mouth and spiritual power is released through our mouth. Unspoken words or thoughts have no power, but spoken words have the power to build and destroy both the hearer and the speaker. James 3:5 says that although the tongue is "a small member, yet it boasts of great things. How great a forest is set ablaze by such a small fire!"

Today, God is encouraging you to keep your mouth from destructive, ungodly, and negative words!

"Set a guard, O Lord, over my mouth; keep watch over the door of my lips!" Psalm 141:3

Ask the Lord to forgive you if you've ever damaged people through your words. It's never too late to receive forgiveness and forgive yourself! Consecrate your mouth to the Lord TODAY and let Him use it for His glory!

Confession:

Even before a word is on my tongue, behold, my Lord knows it altogether. Let the words of my mouth be acceptable in your sight, O Lord, my Rock and my Redeemer. My tongue is a small member but has power to release life. I will set a guard over my mouth and God will watch over the door of my lips. I will guard my mouth, and my tongue and keep myself from calamity. My lips will not speak falsehood, and my tongue will not utter deceit. I am prudent and so I restrain my lips. My speech will always be gracious, seasoned with salt, so that I will answer rightly to each person. I will open my mouth with wisdom, and the teaching of kindness is on my tongue. I will know a time to keep silence, and a time to speak. My lips will pour forth praise, for You teach me Your statutes. My tongue will sing of Your word, for all Your commandments are right (Psalm 19:14; James 3:5; Psalm 141:3; Proverbs 21:23; Job 24:7; Psalm139:4; Proverbs 10:19; Colossians 4:6; Proverbs 31:26; Ecclesiastes 3:7; Ps 119:171,172).

Notes:

5

Keep an Eye on Your Attitude

Do you like being around people who have negative, critical, judgmental, or entitlement attitudes? I'm guessing you'd say no to this! However, you also don't want to be a person who develops these attitudes yourself! In today's devotional, we're going to focus on having right attitudes.

According to the Oxford Dictionary, an attitude is a *"settled way of thinking or feeling about someone or something, typically one that is reflected in a person's behavior"*.

Attitudes can be either good or bad and are completely under our control. While they can be affected by our upbringing and the people with whom we associate, if we are believers, we have no excuse. We are in Christ Jesus, so we are new creations!

> *"You were taught, with regard to your former way of life, to put off your old self, which is being corrupted by its deceitful desires; to be made new in the attitude of your minds; and to put on the new self, created to be like God in true righteousness and holiness." Ephesians 4:22-24*

Philippians 2:5 says that our attitudes *"...should be the same as that of Christ Jesus."* Jesus is our model! He treated everyone with the right attitude at all times. In spite of His sufferings and pain, He handled circumstances, situations and people in a way that always brought glory to our Heavenly Father. He is the Son of God, yet He lived a life of humility.

Humility should not be mistaken for making yourself cheap. True humility is knowing who you are in Christ, serving others selflessly through your gifts, and putting others above yourselves.

14

Take a moment and ask God to help you to carry a right attitude today. May the fragrance of Christ Jesus be diffused through your attitude!

Confession:

I am a new creation in Christ Jesus, made new in the attitude of my mind. I have the mind of Christ in true righteousness and holiness. I am humble and serve others with my gifts. I always put others above myself and my attitudes will bring glory to the name of Jesus. I will be quick to hear, slow to speak and slow to anger. I put away bitterness, wrath, anger, clamor, malice and slander far away from me. I will always think on excellent things worthy of praise and the God of peace will be always with me always (Ephesians 4:22-24; Philippians 2:5; Romans 15:5; Colossians 3:17; Ephesians 4:31; Philippians 4:8-9).

Notes:

6
Mind Renewal: Not an Option

Have you battled recurring thoughts, feelings and habits and haven't been able to experience total victory? You don't have to be ashamed or feel guilty to admit your struggles, as we all have areas where we need to contend for victory. But just as the battle over our minds never ceases, renewing our minds through God's Word should never cease either.

It's important to understand that renewing your mind is an ongoing, lifetime process and not a one-time event. The key to a victorious Christian life begins when we make a commitment to renew our minds according to His Word every single day-no area excluded!

> *"Do not be conformed to this world, but be transformed by the renewal of your mind, that by testing you may discern what is the will of God, what is good and acceptable and perfect." Romans 12:2*

The world's point of view of things totally contradicts God's. For example, in the world, it's the strong who survive. In God's kingdom, however, it's the meek who inherit the earth. Likewise, freedom according to the world's view is to do whatever pleases you with no need for accountability. The Biblical perspective of freedom, however, is to exercise self-control and refuse to defile your spirit, soul and body to live a life that pleases and glorifies God.

> *"The natural person does not accept the things of the Spirit of God, for they are folly to him, and he is not able to understand them because they are spiritually discerned." 1 Corinthians 2:14*

Today, commit your thoughts and actions to God and allow His Word and Spirit to change you. Get ready for the glorious transformation inside and out!

Confession:

I have been bought with a price, the precious blood of Jesus Christ. So, I will glorify God through my body, my actions and my thoughts. I will walk in the Spirit, and I shall not fulfill the lust of the flesh. Where the Spirit of the Lord is, there is freedom; so, I prepare my mind for action and exercise self-control. I will put all my hope in the gracious salvation that will come to me when Jesus Christ is revealed to the world. I choose to live as God's obedient child. I will not slip back into my old ways of living to satisfy my own desires. I didn't know any better then. But now, I am constantly renewed in the spirit of my mind. I can do all things through Christ Who strengthens me (1 Corinthians 6:20; Galatians 5:16; 2 Cor 3:17; 1 Peter 1:13-14; Eph 4:23; Philippians 4:13).

Notes:

7
A Heart Free of Idols

When idols are mentioned, many people tend to think only about carved images. Because of this, real idols of the heart can easily go unnoticed. Anything that takes God's place in your heart is an idol. In 2 Chronicles 19:3, the Lord spoke to Jehoshaphat through Jehu, saying *"There is some good in you, for you have removed the Asheroth from the land and you have set your heart to seek God."* Today, you'll examine your heart to see if there are any idols. If so, destroy and remove them completely!

I was talking to a friend of mine the other day. She said, *"I spent more time in meditating God's Word before I had social media on my cell phone."* In the times we live in, it's easy for any believer to allow social media to become an idol. *"For where your treasure is, there your heart will be also"* Matthew 6:21.

To see God and know His ways, it's vital to check our heart's condition constantly. The Bible says that the pure in heart are blessed, *"...for they will see God."* Matthew 5:8

Only through our hearts can we discern what things are from the Lord. Like eyes with blurry vision, impure hearts can't see spiritual things clearly, and can be deceived. So, let's pray like David prayed in Psalm 26: 2: *"Test me, O LORD, and try me, examine my heart and my mind."*

Today, *"let us draw near with a sincere heart in full assurance of faith, having our hearts sprinkled clean from an evil conscience and our bodies washed with pure water"* (Hebrews 10:22). Accept this challenge and guard your heart with all your might, for it is the wellspring of life (Proverbs 4:23).

Confession:

Just like Jehoshaphat did, I will remove all the idols in my heart and I will seek Him wholeheartedly. I will trust in the LORD with all my heart and lean not on my own understanding. As I delight myself in the LORD, He will give me the desires of my heart. I will flee from all youthful passions and pursue righteousness, faith, love, and peace. I will call on the Lord from a pure heart. With my whole heart, I seek You; my God will not let me wander from His commandments. Just like Ezra had set his heart to study the law of the LORD and to practice it, and to teach His statutes and ordinances in Israel, so will I also set my heart to study His Word and practice it (2 Chron 19:3; Prov. 3:5; Ps 37:4; 2 Tim 2:22; Ps 119:10; Ezra 7:10).

Notes:

8

Clean Hands and a Clear Conscience

"Employees must wash their hands before returning to work"

I 'm sure you've noticed this sign in restaurant bathrooms. It's important to get served by someone who has clean hands! Likewise, the Bible also insists on serving the Lord with clean hands and a clear conscience.

Ask yourself the following questions:

- How many times have I done His ministry work with lazy hands and an insincere heart?
- Have I given my best to glorify God in my job?

The work of our hands will never go unnoticed by the Lord. People may forget what we do for them, but God acknowledges every effort and sacrifice we make to be His hands and feet on the earth.

"The LORD has dealt with me according to my righteousness; according to the cleanness of my hands He has rewarded me." 2 Samuel 22:21

God deserves our best! Whatever we do from this day on, let's do it all for God and not to please people.

"Who may climb the mountain of the LORD? Who may stand in his holy place? Only those whose hands and hearts are pure, who do not worship idols and never tell lies." Psalm 24: 3,4

Seek God's forgiveness and ask the Lord to forgive you for any injustice you might have committed against others. Ask Him to cleanse your hands and purify your heart. The blood of Christ is powerful enough to cleanse us from all sins!

Confession:

The blood of Christ, offered through His Eternal Spirit without blemish to God, cleanses my conscience from dead works to serve the living God. I will not become weary in doing good, for at the proper time I will reap a harvest if I do not give up. I wash my hands in innocence and go to His presence every day. In every place of worship, I will pray with my holy hands lifted to God, free from anger and controversy. I deny ungodliness and worldly desires and will live sensibly, righteously and godly in the present age, looking for the blessed hope and the appearing of the glory of our great God and Savior, Christ Jesus (Galatians 6:9; Psalm 26:6; 1Timothy 2:8; Hebrews 9:14; Titus 2:2-13).

Notes:

9

No Vacancy for Fear, Doubt, and Unbelief

Have fear, doubt or unbelief been camping in your life? These are very destructive forces that need to be served an eviction notice. Today's devotional will help you to post a 'no vacancy' sign before these uninvited guests.

Fear is the opposite of faith. As faith comes by hearing the Word of God or the voice of the Spirit, fear comes by yielding to the world, which is influenced by the demonic realm. To get rid of fear and raise your faith, meditate on and confess the promises of God. *"For God has not given us the spirit of fear; but of power, and of love, and of a sound min"* 2 Timothy 1:7.

Doubt enters your life when you question your faith and are double-minded (asking but not believing you'll receive). The antidote for doubt is to yield to the grace of God and to His Holy Spirit, trust in the finished work on the cross, and trust the promises of God. *James 1:4 says that we should ask in faith "...with no doubting, for the one who doubts is like a wave of the sea that is driven and tossed by the wind."*

> *"Truly, I say to you, whoever says to this mountain, 'Be taken up and thrown into the sea,' and does not doubt in his heart, but believes that what he says will come to pass, it will be done for him". Mark 11:23*

Lastly, unbelief is when you don't trust in God and His ability. The only way out of this is to truly repent and surrender every part of your life to the Lordship of Jesus Christ.

"And he did not do many mighty works there, because of their unbelief." Matthew 13:58

"The father instantly cried out, "I do believe, but help me overcome my unbelief!" Mark 9:24

Pray today that God will completely deliver you from any fear, doubt or unbelief.

Confession:

Even though I walk through the valley of the shadow of death, I will fear no evil, for You are with me; Your rod and Your staff, they comfort me. My God, take hold of my right hand. I will not fear, as You will help me. The Lord is my light and my salvation. I shall not fear. The Lord is the stronghold of my life. I shall not be afraid of anyone. The Lord is my helper; I will not be afraid; no man can do any harm to me. For God has not given me the spirit of fear; but of power, and of love, and of a sound mind. I fear the LORD which is the beginning of all knowledge. From everlasting to everlasting, the Lord's love is with me who fear Him, and His righteousness is with my children's children. When I am afraid, I will trust in Him. In God, whose word I praise, in God I trust; I will not be afraid. What can mortal man do to me? (Psalm 23:4; Isaiah 41:13; Psalm 27:1; Hebrews 13:6; 2 Timothy 1:7: Proverbs 1:7; Ps 103:17; Psalm 56:3-4)

Notes:

_____

_____

_____

_____

10
Marriage is Not Magic

It's God's heart to see our marriages strong, healthy, and divorce-proof. I believe it's His desire that our marriages would proclaim His glory, and especially in these end times.

There is a big attack on marriages today like never before, which is why it's important to have God's perspective for your own marriage and pray for those who are struggling with marital issues. No matter how hard the devil tries to destroy your marriage, however, when it's built on Christ, it will stand the tests and the storms of life. Make sure that your marriage is built upon the bedrock- Christ Jesus.

I encourage you today to forget the mistakes and wrong decisions you've made in the past. Don't let past disappointments rule over you today! Commit your marriage to God and ask Him to forgive you and help you to make wise and godly decisions to honor your marriage covenant. Nothing is impossible with Him!

Take sometime today and do an inventory.

- Is Christ truly the Head of my marriage...and every area of my family?
- As a husband, am I putting my family and my wife's needs above mine? Am I willing to lay down my own life just like Christ did for His Church?
- As a wife, am I truly submitting to the authority of my husband in the family and am I willing not to give up on him, but to pray?

Also remember that as the Bride of Christ, we're all waiting for our Bridegroom, Jesus, to return soon! Let's take the responsibility to honor our covenantal relationship with God. Decide today not to flirt with the world, but to live for Christ. Through Christ, you can do all things!

Confession:

Unless marked to be single, it's God's plan and design for me not to be alone but to cleave with my spouse. We will accomplish more than twice as much as one. We will agree together upon things that concern our marriage and life, and our heavenly Father will do it for us. We will love, respect and care for each other as Christ cares for the Church. We will enjoy life together as ordained by God. As God hates divorce, we hate divorce and we declare that our marriage is divorce-proofed. We will be completely humble and gentle; be patient, bearing with one another in love. We will make every effort to keep the unity of the spirit through the bond of peace. We will be kind to one another, tenderhearted, forgiving one another, even as God in Christ forgave us. We hold our marriage in honor, and our marriage bed will always be kept pure, for God will judge the adulterer and sexually immoral. We know the plans God has for us, plans to prosper us and not to harm us, plans to give us hope and a future (Genesis 2:18,24, Matthew 19:4-6, Ephesians 5:21-23; Ecclesiastes 9:9; Malachi 2:16; Ephesians 4:2-3, 32; Hebrews 13:4; Jeremiah 29:11).

Notes:

11
Use Your Rod

God's intention for marriage between a man and a woman is to bring forth a generation that will choose to worship Him and serve Him willingly. Although the devil hates our children and fights hard to destroy them, God is there to keep watch over them. Our part is to equip the next generation to stand against the enemy of their souls.

Every child should be disciplined, trained and nurtured about the things of the Lord at home. Our children belong to the Lord, so when disciplining a child, we have to have God's heart. We want to be very careful not to bring fear of men but help them to fear only God.

When Moses stood before the Red Sea and panicked, God asked him what was in his hand. He asked Moses to use the rod and split the sea. As parents, we should learn to use the 'rod', which is His Word, to speak into our children's lives.

Are you struggling or panicking with your child or children's behaviors and attitudes? Use your rod! Are you concerned about the choices of your grown-up children? Use your rod! No matter where your children are in their walk with the Lord, use your rod! God will bring the deliverance!

Let's consecrate and surrender the fruits of our womb to the Lord. Let's seek God's wisdom to parent them. Just Like Joshua confessed, let's also confess that as for me and my house, we will serve the Lord!

Confession:

My children are a heritage from the Lord, the fruit of the womb a reward. I will train up my children in the way they should go; even when they are old, they will not depart from it. I will not spare the rod, because I love them. I will be diligent to discipline them just like my heavenly Father would discipline me. I will take time to teach them, talk to them, when I sit in the house, and when I walk by the way, and when I lie down, and when I rise. I need wisdom to train up, discipline and nurture my children. I will ask our generous God, and He will give it to me. My children will live and declare the glory of God (Ps 127:3; Prov 22:6; Prov 13:24; Deut 11;19; James 1:5; Psalm 118:17).

Notes:

12

Get Rid of Termites

In general, forgiving others is one of the easiest things to say, but can actually be a very difficult thing to do. However, when you understand the truth about forgiving others and how it benefits you, you'll want to make sure you're doing this continuously!

Unforgiveness is a root cause of bitterness, anger, rejection, insecurity, poor self-esteem, grief, pain, hatred, revenge, and even many sicknesses. You can be completely released from this demonic stronghold when you forgive those who have hurt you.

Imagine an invasion of termites in your home. If they go unnoticed, they can eat up your entire house! Likewise, unforgiveness that isn't dealt with can consume your physical and emotional well-being.

How do you know if you're carrying unforgiveness in your heart? It's a possibility if you're experiencing any of the following symptoms:

- You feel like you're in an emotional prison or emotional roller coaster.
- You're experiencing torment.
- You're battling with a long-term sickness, and no matter what you do, it's still there.
- You have many unanswered prayers.
- You're not blessed in the ways you should be, according to what the Bible promises.

If any of these are present in your life, take the first step to healing and restoration by deciding to get rid of these *"termites"* of unforgiveness before they completely destroy your life. You can do it! Yes, through Christ you can do all things!

Choose to forgive those who have wounded and caused deep pain in your life. Write their names. Forgive them and bless them in Jesus' Name. Release them to the Lord. He will fight for you!

Confession:

I choose to forgive others with the help of God. I forgive everyone who has spoken or worked or prayed against me. Having forgiven them, I bless them in the Name of the Lord. As I forgive others, I am totally forgiven by God and I am free. I forgive others, so my prayers will not be hindered. I will continually bear with others; forgive them as the Lord forgave me. I am rid of all bitterness, rage, anger, brawling, slander and malice. I will be compassionate to others. I choose to love others, as love is patient and kind, does not envy or boast, and is not arrogant or rude. I will not insist upon my own way, become irritable or resentful, but I rejoice in truth, believing all things, hope all things and will endure all things. Jesus has set me free! I am free indeed (Matthew 6:14-15; Matthew 5:24; Colossians 3:13; Ephesians 4:31-32; 1 Corinthians 13:4-7; John 8:36).

Notes:

13
Deal with the Root

As we align ourselves with God's plan for our lives in this season, we're going to take a look at sickness and disease from God's perspective.

Although we cannot deny the pain and the suffering of people around us and may have even lost loved ones to deadly diseases, it's very important to keep our faith and trust in God and His Word. He is not the author of sin, sickness or disease.

Since we are triune beings, we need to deal with our spirits, souls, and bodies to be in good health. We must also know that sickness can be due to other reasons as well, such as sin, demonic oppression, curses, or natural causes. Even unforgiveness is a barrier to healing and blessings. These are some of the invisible barriers to healing and deliverance, and we need to deal each of these roots appropriately.

- Sin: Stay away from sin, which could bring sickness to your body. When we truly repent and turn around, the blood of Jesus cleanses us from all sins.

- Curses: Recognize it and appropriate redemption through the finished work of Jesus. Jesus hung on the cross as a curse and redeemed us from the curse and released us into the blessings (Galatians 3:13,14). Deuteronomy chapters 27 & 28 give insight into curses and blessings. Take the time to read it today.

- Demonic Oppression: Jesus destroyed the works of the devil. When we surrender to the Lord and resist the devil, he will flee from us and we are free, as Jesus sets us free. Many sicknesses are healed when we get delivered from demonic oppressions.

- Natural Causes: Healthy food, rest and physical exercise are important for your body to function. Even a car needs proper gas, oil and rest to drive well for a long time. Refrain from unhealthy foods and try to make the best choices to help your body do all that it was created to do. Proper rest will heal your mind and body.

With God's help and our sincere efforts, we can break through to see the full manifestation of our healing. His will is for us to prosper in all things and be in good health, which is why He took all our sickness, diseases, pain and cares. By His stripes we are healed!

Confession:

I have repented to God and He has forgiven all my sins. His blood has cleansed me from all sins. I am redeemed, cleansed, sanctified and set apart by the blood of Jesus. I have forgiven others and so I am free in Christ Jesus. Jesus took my pain and bore my suffering, He was pierced for my transgressions, He was crushed for my iniquities; the punishment that brought me peace was on Him, and His wounds healed me. I am healed by the stripes of Jesus. I am redeemed from all generational curses by the sacrificial death of Jesus on the cross. Now I receive the blessings of the Lord. I rebuke the devil and he flees from me and I am free, as Jesus has set me free. Since my body is the temple of the Holy Spirit, I stand resolute to eat healthy, rest well and exercise. I can do all things through Christ Jesus. I will live and declare the glory of God (1 John 1: 9 & 7; Ephesians 1:7; Hebrews 13:12; Matthew 6:14-15; Isaiah 53:4,5; Galatians 3:13-14; 1 John 3:8; John 8:36; 1 Corinthians 6:19; Philippians 3:14; Psalm 118:17).

Notes:

14
Blessed to be a Blessing

You can't give what you don't have. That's why God wants His children to be blessed, so they can be a blessing!

The Bible has never been against God's people being wealthy. In fact, it's God who gives us power to get wealth. There is nothing wrong in having wealth as long as the wealth does not have you. Remember this promise from Deuteronomy 8:18: *"You shall remember the LORD your God: for it is he that gives you power to get wealth, that he may establish his covenant which he swore to your fathers, as it is this day."*

Let's ask the Lord to forgive our ignorance and lack of understanding towards wealth. God wants us to be blessed. He doesn't want us to accumulate wealth, but to use it to bless others instead. 2 Corinthians 9:10 says that God gives seed to the sower. He also promises in Psalm 1 that when we meditate on His Word day and night, we'll be prosperous.

Today let's consecrate our desires, ideas, thoughts, and efforts to become wealthy. Let's believe God to break any poverty spirit in our lives and cause a shift in our mindset. May the Lord bless our efforts and bless all that is according to His will!

Confession:

I will bless the Lord, who daily loads me with benefits, even the God of my salvation. The earth is the LORD's, and the fullness thereof; the world, and they that dwell therein. The LORD shall increase me more and more, me and my children. By humility and the fear of the LORD are riches, and honor, and life. I will keep His words and do them, so I may prosper in all that I do. *"Blessed be the God and Father of our Lord Jesus Christ, who hath blessed us with all spiritual blessings in heavenly places in Christ."* (Psalms 68:19; Psalms 24:1; Psalms 115:14; Proverbs 22:4 Deuteronomy 29:9; Ephesians 1:3)

Notes:

15

Prayer is a Missile

"Don't forget: Prayer Is a Missile!"
Sam Dewald

Prayer is a great luxury with which every believer has been bestowed. Jesus said in Matthew 21:22 that if we would believe, we would receive whatever we ask for in prayer. This means that there are no limitations as long as it agrees with His will.

Long-range ballistic missiles travel thousands of miles yet are still able to hit their targets with 100% accuracy. Prayer is like a spiritual ballistic missile, but more powerful. It has more than 100% accuracy and unlimited range.

Along with the blessing of asking and receiving, prayer is a means of fellowship with God. We listen to Him to understand His will and then we pray for His revealed will to be accomplished.

God always answers our prayers when we ask and move in faith. Prayer is activated and brings results only by our faith actions. Many of us ask in faith, but either we don't take corresponding actions or are unable to wait and endure until the answer comes. Remember, God does everything beautifully in His perfect timing-He will never be late or too early.

Consecrate your prayer life today. Ask God to give you His anointing and His grace to pray like never before, as well as the faith to believe for greater things this year.

Confession:

The LORD is near to me as I call upon him in truth. I am blessed with the powerful tool of prayer, which brings all that I ask in Jesus Name. My prayers are always answered as I ask and believe and move in corresponding faith action. I will pray in the Spirit, as He helps me in my weakness and intercedes for me. I will not be anxious about anything, but in every situation, I will give thanks and pray to my God. I will devote myself to prayer, being watchful and thankful. I always triumph as my God answers my prayers above all I ask or think. I am an overcomer in Christ Jesus (Ps 145:18; Matthew 21:22; James 2:17; Romans 8:26; Philippians 4:6; Colossians 4:2; Ephesians 3:20; 1 John 5:4).

Notes:

16
Called to Know His Word

A re you wondering what's in God's heart for your life? Are you looking for an answer or direction for the next step? No matter what you're seeking, you can go right to the source of all counsel and wisdom...the Word of God! Psalm 119:105 says that His Word is *"a lamp to our feet and a light to our path."*

When it seems like everything around you is shaking and falling, run to the unshakable, firm foundation of the Word of God. When you feel like tossed by the waves of this life, remember that He is a shield to those who trust and take refuge in Him (Proverbs 30:5). Also, Psalm 37: 31 states that when *"the Law of God is in our heart, our feet do not slip."*

The Word of God is the most creative and effective tool He's given us. When we speak and release His Word in whatever situation we find ourselves, the Word will create, destroy, or restore according to the demand of the situation. In other words, it will accomplish the purpose for which it was sent. Why? Because God's words are alive and full of power, active, operative, energizing, and effective. Jesus declared in Matthew 24:35 that *"Heaven and earth will pass away, but My words will not pass away."*

Decide today to study the Scriptures and do what they say. Base every decision you make this year according to the Word of God. Decide that if the Bible says not to do something, you will also say no. Learn to replace personal egocentric motives and words of 'I want', 'I think', I feel' by God's Word and His will. This is the best way to defuse the plans of the enemy against your life and walk victoriously!

If you haven't been reading the Word like you should, seek

forgiveness from the Lord today. Consecrate your Bible reading routine to the Lord. Ask Him to help you read in the morning and in the night consistently, so you can prosper in your spirit, soul, and body like never before. (Joshua 1:8)

Confession:

God's Word is ever settled in heavens. His Word is alive and full of power making it active, operative, energizing, and effective and is sharper than any two-edged sword. I will use it to destroy the enemies' plan and to open and close doors. Since His Word is a lamp unto my feet, I will take every step based on the Word and I will do the right things at the right time. His Word is laid up in my heart; therefore, I will not sin. His Word is like a medicine. I will release it and it will bring health to my whole body. To every situation and difficulty I face, I will proclaim the Word of God. God's Word goes forth out of My mouth: it shall not return to Me void, but it shall accomplish that which I please and purpose, and it shall prosper in the thing for which I sent it. I will declare the works of the Lord and bring Him glory (Psalm 119:89; Hebrews 4:12; Psalm 119:105; Psalm 119:11; Proverbs 4:22; Mark 11:23-25; Isaiah 55:11; Psalm 118:17).

Notes:

17
Desire the Gifts

Would you ever say 'no' to a gift? Probably not, right? Did you know that God also wants His children to learn to receive gifts from Him?

According to the Merriam Webster Dictionary, a *"gift»* is defined as *"something voluntarily transferred by one person to another without compensation."* The gifts that God gives us are spiritual gifts and are very powerful. Sadly, not many of us are aware of them or use them as God intended. The Bible, however, encourages us to earnestly seek for the gifts because they are given by Him to help the Body of Christ (and not merely for personal gain).

To be fruitful and powerful in these end times, every believer should desire to receive the gifts of the Spirit and use them. God has voluntarily transferred His power to us through His gifts of the Spirit, which are discussed in 1 Corinthians 12. How we need these gifts to live a successful life and help others! When we exercise our gifts, we deeply affect both the spiritual and natural realm.

Ask the Lord today for spiritual gifts. One of these gifts is the Holy Spirit. If you have not received the gift of the baptism of the Holy Spirit yet, ask Him to fill you now (Acts 2:38). Recognize the gifts you've been blessed with and consecrate them to the Lord. How exciting life will become when you exercise your gifts! Begin to use them for God's glory this year!

Confession:

I am a believer in Jesus Christ. I have repented and baptized in the name of Jesus Christ for the remission of sins: I shall receive the gift of the Holy Spirit, for the promise is to me and to my children. My Father God has created me with unique gifts and I will use them. I eagerly desire the greater spiritual gifts. The spiritual gifts are given to me for the profit of all. As a member of the body of Christ, I will use them to bring freedom and liberty to others. I will prophesy, minister, teach, exhort, give liberally, lead with all diligence, and will be hospitable. I will use the spiritual gifts manifested in me through the Holy Spirit to minister to others for the profit of all (Acts 2:38; 1 Corinthians 12:31; Romans 12:6; 1 Corinthians 12:7; Romans 12:6-8; 1 Corinthians 12:4-11).

Notes:

18
Called to Bear Fruit

T he minute we accept Christ as our Savior, we become a new creation and all old things are passed away. If that's the case, though, why do we still get angry and impatient at times? Why do we find ourselves unable to exercise self-control the way we ought to?

The reason for this is because our sinful nature does not disappear automatically. We actually begin a new journey with the Holy Spirit to crucify our carnal nature, so we can let the fruit of the Spirit grow every day. It is an ongoing, never ending process.

Unlike the gifts of the Spirit, the fruit of the Spirit is not instantaneous. It starts as a seed and develops and matures as we spend time with the Lord.

> *"Thefruitofthespiritislove,joy,peace,patience,kindness, goodness, faithfulness, gentleness and self-control."*
> *Galatians 5:22*

If you look at this passage, you'll notice that there are not nine fruits of the Spirit, but just one fruit (love) with nine components in it.

This same chapter in Galatians also mentions the works of the flesh, which area easy to identify. It's important that as you continue to walk with the Lord, you make every failure an opportunity to learn and grow-don't allow condemnation to set in. But also, be careful not to give excuses or let your flesh dominate. Through the help of the Holy Spirit, you can become strong and bear fruit, every day, in every circumstance.

Today, ask the Lord to help you grow in the fruit of the Spirit. Thank Him for the growth in you. Desire to get closer to the Lord and learn to abide in Jesus. You are called to bear fruit and represent Jesus in these last days, for we will be known by our fruit and not just by our gifts.

Confession:

Today, I confess that I have love, which is patient, and kind. I will not envy, and I will not boast, I will not be proud. I will not dishonor others. I will not be self-seeking, and I will not be easily angered. I will keep no record of wrongs. I will be joyful in hope, patient in affliction, faithful in prayer. The LORD will give me His strength, and He will bless me with peace. As the branch cannot bear fruit by itself unless it abides in the vine, neither can I, unless I abide in Jesus. Jesus is the vine; I am the branch. As I abide in Him, I will bear much fruit, for apart from Him I can do nothing (I Corinthians 13:1-3; Philippians 4:4; Ps 29:11; John 15: 4-5).

Notes:

19

Called to Serve While You Lead

The call on every follower of Christ is to serve and lead, as Christ did. Jesus said that whoever wanted to be great needed to learn to be a servant of all (Mark 10:43). A servant leader is one who will take time to lead, train and build others up. The term *"serving"* is not always popular as it takes humility, love and strength. However, this type of leadership reflects how Jesus led as He walked this earth. Like Him, we are called to serve our Father and lead His people to Him.

> *"When He had washed their feet and put on His outer garments and resumed His place, He said to them, "Do you understand what I have done to you? You call me Teacher and Lord, and you are right, for so I am. If I then, your Lord and Teacher, have washed your feet, you also ought to wash one another's feet. For I have given you an example, that you also should do just as I have done to you.""* John 13:12-15

Are you ready to lead His flock and serve them as well? Jesus did everything that He saw His Father do. He had no self-agenda but came to fulfill Father's plan. God is looking for servant leaders who are willing to serve Him at any cost, without pride, hidden agendas, or selfish motives. Will you say yes to Him?

Confession:

For even the Son of Man came not to be served but to serve, and to give His life as a ransom for many, I also will serve the Lord by serving others and will lead them to Christ. I will do nothing from rivalry or conceit, but in humility count others more significant than myself. I will not look only to my own interests, but also to the interests of others. I have the mind of Christ. I will lead with humility to lead, build and train others to fulfill their destiny. I will follow the leading of the Holy Spirit in all circumstances and will be ready to serve others as the situation demands. I will serve the Lord as I serve others (Mark 10:45; Acts 20:28; Phil 2: 3-8; 1 Corinthians 9:22; Ephesians 6:7).

Notes:

20
Yoke-Breaking Anointing

When God created Adam and Eve, they were free and had intimate fellowship with God, which was the main purpose of their creation. Satan hates to see people who freely worship and serve their Creator. So, he deceived them into sinning against God, which broke their fellowship and put them under his yoke. Mankind is now under Satan's yoke and controlled by him.

A yoke is an arched device formerly laid on the neck of a defeated person. When someone had a yoke on their neck, they would have no freedom and would be treated cruelly and unfairly. The devil uses his yokes of addiction, religious strongholds, witchcraft, and many other yokes to keep people in bondage.

The Bible declares that the anointing of the Holy Spirit will break the yoke. The anointing of the Holy Spirit destroys the yoke of the enemy (Isaiah 10:27) and empowers you to accomplish what God has called you to do and advance His kingdom (Isaiah 61:1). It also teaches and directs you into the right way (1 John 2:27) and breaks open new doors and closed doors (Micah 2:12-13).

We often think that the anointing is just for Christian ministry, but it's also much needed for our everyday lives. The only way to destroy the works of the enemy is by operating under the anointing of the Holy Spirit. Where the Spirit of the Lord is, there is freedom. Jesus came to destroy the works of the devil. As the enemy works against us constantly, we should desire to grow more in the anointing because when the anointing increases, the yoke is broken.

The three things that sets people free are the Holy Spirit, the truth, and the Son of God. The Bible declares that you will know the truth and the truth will set you free (John 8:32); that where the Spirit of the Lord is, there is freedom (2 Corinthians 3:17); and whom the Son sets free is free indeed (John 8:36).

Let us consecrate ourselves today and ask God to anoint us. We will do greater things this year than ever before, as the anointing increases.

Confession:

The baptism of the Holy Spirit is for me and my children. As I seek the Lord and wait on Him, I will receive more anointing. The anointing breaks the yoke of the enemy against my life, so I now live in total freedom. I am anointed to preach the good news, to heal the brokenhearted and those oppressed by the devil, and to set the captives free. God has anointed me; I now know the truth and walk in freedom. The One Who breaks open goes before me to open the closed doors and to open new doors. I am powerful, blessed and fruitful as I continuously seek the Lord and as the anointing grows (Acts 2:39; Isaiah 10:27; Isaiah 61:1; Acts 10:38; 1 John 2:27; Micah 2:12-13).

Notes:

21

Ready, Set, it's Time to Go

What an incredible journey it's been! We've arrived at the last day of our 21-day journey toward consecration and preparation. Though this journey is closing, my prayer is that you've received the wisdom you need to stay on the right track. As you keep moving, taking every step by faith and not by sight, you will eventually get to the destination God has planned for you.

When weariness, sickness, doubt, fear, unbelief or any other weapon of the enemy strikes you along the way, always remember God's promises. Arise, shake off the dust and declare, *"The One Who has begun a work in me is faithful to complete it!"* Yes, He has promised that He will never leave nor forsake you!

Let your mountains hear you speak to them to be moved and be gone in Jesus Name! Let Goliath hear you say, *"Who are you, you uncircumcised Philistine, mocking my God? I come in the Name of the Most High God and I will slay you!"* Let Jericho's walls crumble and fall as they hear your praise and worship! The Lord will send the wind and split the sea, as you keep holding the rod, His Word, stretched forth.

When you encounter new battles, allow the Lord to train your fingers, for He has promised victory. Through Him, you can run against a troop and leap over a wall! He is ABLE!!! Absolutely nothing is IMPOSSIBLE for Him!!! Learn to fix your eyes only upon the Lord. He is the Great I AM!!!

Today, hear Him say to you:
"My child, I AM... your Healer; I AM... your Savior;
I AM... your Deliverer; I AM... your Refuge; I AM... your Fortress;
I AM... your Redeemer; I AM... your Provider; I AM... your
Protector;

*I AM... your Hope; I AM your very present help
in the time of trouble;
I AM Peace; I AM Love and I AM with you...Always!!!"
So, arise and shine for your time has come! Go forth in the
Name of the Lord and do great exploits this year!*

Confession:

I do not claim that I have already succeeded or have already become perfect. I keep striving to win the prize for which Christ Jesus Himself has already won for me. I forget what is behind me and do my best to reach what is ahead. I run straight toward the goal to win the prize, which is God's call through Christ Jesus to the life above. Therefore, I prepare my mind for action, keep a clear head, and set my hope completely on the grace. I can do all things through Christ who strengthens me. I will leap over a wall and run against an army. I am more than a conqueror in Christ Jesus. He continues to lead me along in Christ's triumphal procession. Though I may walk through fire and water, nothing will harm me; He will lead me to a broad place. In the Name of the Lord, I move forward and will declare His works to my generation in my job, business and ministry! (Philippians 3:12-14; 1 Peter 1:13; Philippians 4:13; Psalm 18:29; Romans 8:37; 2 Corinthians 2:14; Isaiah 43:2; Psalm 18:19; Psalm 145:4)

Notes:

_____

_____

_____

_____

_____

Other book by the author

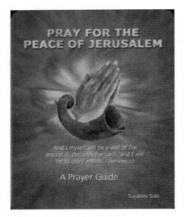

Psa 122:6 Pray for the peace of Jerusalem: "May they prosper who love you." Psa 122:7 "Peace be within your walls, Prosperity within your palaces"

This prayer booklet is key for a prosperous and peaceful life. Many of us may do not know how to pray for the nation of God? What are the prayer needs of the nation of God? While I was living as a family in Israel, I have seen and heard many things and based on that and as per the leading of the Holy Spirit, I have prepared 31 prayer points for a whole month.

To thank the Lord for what he has done to and through the nation and people of Israel, I have prepared 31 praise points.

As we pray with the burden for the nation of Israel it is sure that all the blessings due to us will overtake us.

Mat 6:33 "But seek first the kingdom of God and His righteousness, and all these things shall be added to you."

About the Author

Suganthi Sam is an ordained minister and has been working alongside her husband, Sam, in the ministry for the past 17 years. She is a graduate of Christ for the Nations Institute, Dallas, TX, from The Advanced School of Children and Family Ministry. She is ordained by the Christ for the Nations – Fellowship of Members and Churches.

Suganthi is also the author of the powerful prayer booklet and guide entitled **Pray for the Peace of Jerusalem**. Her passion is family, children and intercession, and to see the souls and nations transformed and revived.

Sam and Suganthi have been married for 22 years and are blessed with a son and daughter, Immanuel and Irene.

www.samdewald.org • 1-888-958-6597 • info@samdewald.org
©2019 Sam Dewald Ministries

50407458R00031

Made in the USA
Columbia, SC
09 February 2019